LITT

NAUGHTY GAMES

Sadie Cayman

summersdale

THE LITTLE BOOK OF NAUGHTY GAMES

First published as *Very Naughty Games* in 2011

Summersdale Publishers Ltd
46 West Street
Chichester
West Sussex
PO19 1RP
UK

www.summersdale.com

Printed and bound in Malta

ISBN: 978-1-84953-641-7

Substantial discounts on bulk quantities of Summersdale books are available to corporations, professional associations and other organisations. For details contact general enquiries: telephone: +44 (0) 1243 771107, fax: +44 (0) 1243 786300 or email: enquiries@summersdale.com.

Contents

Introduction

Boring sex lives are for your parents, vicars, that woman who runs the PTA and anyone who gets excited by a yellow-breasted cockatoo. Yours may be going through a dry patch, a rough patch or an unusually wet patch, but no matter how much of a sexpert or novice you may be, there's no harm in spicing things up with some super-fun, super-sexy sex games. So congratulations for picking up this book, and welcome.

This sexy stocking-full of titillating treats should get you hot under the collar and ready for some stripped-down, hard-core bedroom action. From frisky foreplay teasers to downright dirty duvet dalliances, there's something in here for every sexual occasion. So get your 'shagging' underwear on (boys, make sure it's clean!) and prepare to take it off not long after, 'cause it's time to play!

Strictly for adults only!

I GENERALLY AVOID TEMPTATION UNLESS I CAN'T RESIST IT.

MAE WEST

FLIRTY
Fun

HUSSY ROULETTE

You will need

A BOTTLE

A PAIR OF HANDCUFFS

A SPANKING TOOL

A BUCKET OF ICE CUBES

NAUGHTINESS RATING ▼ ▼ ▼

Place the bottle in the centre of the room à la 'Spin the Bottle' and position the other objects at equal distances around the circle. Take turns with your partner to spin the bottle. If it rests pointed at a 'safe zone', where there are no objects, the other person takes their turn at spinning. If not, follow the rules below...

RAUNCHY RULES

If the bottle's pointed at...
... the handcuffs, cuff your partner to the nearest static object and do whatever you want to them.
... the spanking tool, your partner (or yourself, it's your choice!) gets a light spanking for their bad behaviour.
... the bucket of ice cubes, then cool your partner down with an ice cube down the back or in their pants.

WET 'N' WILD

You will need

WATER PISTOLS
BUCKETS
BALLOONS
PLENTY OF WATER!*

*Use warm water – you don't want to catch hypothermia, and avoiding shrinkage in the nether-regions is always a good thing.

NAUGHTINESS RATING 🩲 🩲

Find somewhere where nudity and water sports go hand in hand – such as a back garden that's not overlooked. Deck yourself out in your skimpiest lingerie/most manly man-pants and a tight-fitting white T-shirt. Select your watery weapons of choice – no, boys, not that – (water pistols, water bombs, a good old-fashioned bucket) and fill them up. Take it in turns to ask each other sexy questions, to test how well you know each other; what's my favourite position, where's the craziest place we've ever had sex, for example. For every question your partner gets wrong, you get to give them a good squirting. Keep going till your underwear's good and see-through.

PLEASURE HUNT

You will need

YOUR OWN CLOTHES
SOME SEXY UNDERWEAR
CANDLES
ROSE PETALS
CARDS AND ENVELOPES
A PEN

*This game involves a bit of forward planning, but it'll be worth it. That's a promise!

NAUGHTINESS RATING ▼ ▼

Before your partner arrives for your date, hide the clothes you've been wearing that day (including your underwear) in different locations around the house. Write out clues that will lead your partner from your coat, to your skirt/trousers, to your shirt, etc. and place them in envelopes with each item of clothing (the first clue to your coat is taped to the front door). The last clue (with your pants) should lead your lover to a spot you've decided to recline naked, surrounded by rose petals and candles. They've found the pleasure chest!

Titillating Tip

Try to make the clues as enticing as possible to keep
your partner interested, and to ensure they don't just go
looking for you round the house.

MY BEST CHAT-UP LINE?
'LET ME SHOW YOU A FEW
OF MY JUDO HOLDS.'

HONOR BLACKMAN

SEX
For All
SEASONS

BE MY VALENTINE

Best day to play

ST VALENTINE'S DAY

You will need

20 SMALL PIECES OF PAPER

A PEN

A BOX OF CHOCOLATES

NAUGHTINESS RATING ▼ ▼ ▼

Before your partner arrives for their Valentine's treat, draw hearts on ten of the pieces of paper. Lay blankets and cushions on the floor (light a few candles and put on some sexy tunes to get you in the mood) and place all the pieces of paper face down on the blanket.

Get naked with your partner and sit, without touching, on the blanket. Each choose one piece of paper and turn it over. If the piece of paper has a heart on it, you must select a chocolate from the box and eat it off your partner's body (which part is up to you). If you both pick a heart then you get double the pleasure! If neither of you pick a heart, you must wait until the end of the song that's playing before you can pick again. Use this time to get your partner hot and bothered – no mouth action allowed but touch them all you want. After each round replace the pieces of paper and mix them up. Play until you either run out of chocolates or you'd rather be nibbling on each other.

FLIPPIN' STICKY

Best day to play

PANCAKE DAY

You will need

PANCAKE BATTER
A SHALLOW FRYING PAN
A BOTTLE OF POURING SYRUP
TWO APRONS

NAUGHTINESS RATING ▼ ▼ ▼

Wearing nothing but aprons, take it in turns with your partner to cook a pancake. Whoever goes first must then see how many times you can flip the pancake without dropping it/breaking it/getting it stuck to the ceiling, etc. After each successful flip they receive a seductive kiss from the other person. Their turn ends when they fail to flip the pancake. If they manage to successfully flip the pancake five times in a row then they must pour syrup over the other person's naked body and lick it off. To crank up the rude rating a notch, insist that your partner flips their next pancake in the buff. There's nothing sexier than a truly naked chef!

There's no denying food and sex go well together, but make sure you've got tasty options your partner's into. Don't feel like getting doused in sticky syrup? How about strawberry sauce, chocolate spread or squirty cream?

LEAD ME NOT INTO TEMPTATION. I CAN FIND THE WAY MYSELF.

RITA MAE BROWN

GET THE TENT UP

Best days to play

WHEN YOU'RE CAMPING OR AT A
MUSIC FESTIVAL

You will need

A TENT
TWO SLEEPING BAGS

NAUGHTINESS RATING 👙 👙

During your camping trip or weekend at the festival, take some time out with your partner and retreat to your tent. Zip yourselves up in your sleeping bags, fully clothed, and then race to see who can get naked first without getting out of the sleeping bag. Whoever can present a full pile of their clothes outside their sleeping bag first is the winner.

RAUNCHY RULES

Since you went to the trouble of getting yourselves naked, the winner should really receive some kind of reward. Emerge from your sleeping bags and get cosy. Whoever undressed the fastest should then be on the receiving end of the best oral sex EVER!

Had enough beer and boogying for one day? Text your partner/cute mate/person you just met in the crowd and invite them back to your tent for some daytime playtime.

REMEMBER, REMEMBER TO WEAR YOUR SUSPENDERS!

Best day to play

BONFIRE NIGHT

You will need

A PAIR OF HANDCUFFS

SOME SEXY LINGERIE

A BLINDFOLD

NAUGHTINESS RATING

Bring the explosions to the bedroom with this mischievous Bonfire Night game. Put your sexy lingerie on under your clothes. Handcuff your naughty partner to a chair in just their underwear. Proceed to ask them to recall details about your relationship (the saucier the better). For every detail they recall correctly you will remove one item of your clothing, but if they answer incorrectly you will blindfold them, and the game will continue without them being able to enjoy the view. Any further wrong answers will result in your putting clothes back on. They are handcuffed throughout unless, during the game, you hear fireworks exploding outside. If this happens, then you must un-cuff them and let them finish undressing you themselves.

Titillating Tip

Some possible details to ask them to remember are:

💋 Where did we have our first kiss?

💋 What flavour ice cream do I most like to lick off your body?

💋 What sexual position turns me on the most?

💋 What do I prefer – being spanked or being massaged?

STOCKING STUFFERS

Best day to play

CHRISTMAS DAY

You will need

LOTS OF KINKY LITTLE TREATS
WRAPPED UP IN FESTIVE PAPER
A SACK/PILLOWCASE

How to Play

NAUGHTINESS RATING ▼ ▼ ▼

Find a time of the day when you're alone with your partner (make sure there's no chance grandma can walk in on the game). Stuff all the presents into the sack and invite your partner to pick them out one by one. For each gift they have 10 seconds to identify what is in the package, but are only allowed one guess. Then they must open the gift and reveal its true identity. If they are correct then they get to keep the gift to use later in the evening; if not, then they must hand it over to you. Be really outrageous in your selection of items. If you're normally fairly reserved in the bedroom throw a few random toys in there that shock you, you never know, if he guesses right you might get a Christmas present you didn't expect.

Some stocking stuffer suggestions are: a vibrator, lubricant, porn movie, blindfold and massage oils.

BE NAUGHTY – SAVE SANTA A TRIP.

ANONYMOUS

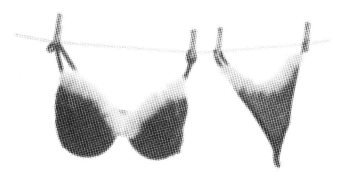

EAT
Me!

STRAWBERRIES AND CREAMY

You will need

SQUIRTY CREAM
STRAWBERRRIES

NAUGHTINESS RATING ▼ ▼ ▼

Surprise your partner by preparing them a tasty dessert.
Strip down and squirt cream onto your nipples,
bellybutton and anywhere else that takes your fancy.
While lying down on the kitchen table, carefully position
strawberries on the creamy areas, and call for your lover
to come in and lick you all over.

RAUNCHY RULES

Your partner has 10 minutes to eat as many strawberries
as they can (while giving you a good licking in the
process). For every strawberry they eat you'll give them a
little lick back afterwards. And remember, not everyone's
big on cream – chocolate mousse is another great tasty
treat that might get them going.

If things are getting too sticky, take your naked body (and your partner) off to the shower, so you can rinse off.

FONDUE FULL-FRONTAL

You will need

A FEW BARS OF CHOCOLATE

TWO SPATULAS

DICE

NAUGHTINESS RATING ▼ ▼ ▼ ▼

Melt a big bowl of dark chocolate (milk, if you like, but dark's an aphrodisiac) and sit down naked in the middle of the room. Each of you will need a plastic spatula and a die. Roll the dice, and whoever gets the highest number is allowed to paint one body part of the other person. When you're both good and chocolatey, stop spreading, then, whoever rolls the highest number can demand which body part the other person licks.

RAUNCHY RULES

For alternative game-play, ditch the spatulas and smear the chocolate on with your fingers.

Titillating Tip

Don't overdo it with the licking. Chocolate tastes good, but you don't want to make yourself sick when things are about to get raunchy!

HOOCHIE HOOPLA

You will need

PEANUT M&Ms
SMARTIES
SQUIRTY CREAM
RING DOUGHNUTS

How to Play

NAUGHTINESS RATING ▼ ▼ ▼ ▼

Strip down to your underwear and stand a few metres away from your partner. You have 20 attempts each to achieve all of the following:

💋 Throw an M&M into your partner's mouth = 2 points

💋 Throw a Smartie into your partner's mouth = 4 points

💋 Squirt cream onto your partner's torso = 6 points

💋 Land a doughnut anywhere on your partner's body (head, feet, resting on a boob) = 8 points

NB: Anyone who can successfully toss a doughnut onto their partner's penis scores 10 points for their awesome skills! (If your partner is a lady, then the 10-pointer is awarded for successful finger-looping.)

SEX ON TELEVISION CAN'T HURT YOU UNLESS YOU FALL OFF.

ANONYMOUS

LIGHTS,
Camera,
ACTION!

SEX ON SCREEN

You will need

A COUPLE OF YOUR FAVOURITE SEXY MOVIES
SOME SERIOUS ACTING SKILLS

How to Play

NAUGHTINESS RATING ▼ ▼ ▼ ▼

If you've never been to drama school, this one might take a bit of practice. Have a few blush-crushing drinks and put on a sexy movie to watch together. Decide who will go first before the title sequence fades, and then when the first sexy scene appears, watch it intently, press pause and perform it on (or for) your partner. Then press play and let the movie continue.

RAUNCHY RULES

You set the rules for what will be included (i.e. kissing, fondling, spanking, oral sex, nudity, stripping, etc.). If either one of you doesn't want to act out a particular sequence they must forfeit by performing a task decided by their partner. (Examples include: giving the other person a foot massage, doing some kind of domestic chore or downing a shot of tequila.)

Quick Change

To mix it up, take a break from acting and make out with each other whenever a character in the movie says an agreed word, such as 'Knickers!'

PEEP SHOW

You will need

BOX WITH COIN SLOT
SPARE CHANGE
MUSIC

NAUGHTINESS RATING ▼ ▼ ▼

Sit your partner on the sofa next to a conveniently placed box with a slot marked 'Insert Coins Here'. Pop on some sexy music and wait for them to pay up. Donations of different amounts will result in different performances, which you should make your customer aware of (see below)*. Their final amount donated will equal the number of minutes you spend pleasuring them after they're all excited and out of pocket.

💋 10p = reveal a sexy secret about yourself

💋 20p = describe a sexual fantasy

💋 50p = do a sexy dance (clothed)

💋 £1 = flash some flesh

💋 £2 = flash a little more

💋 £5 = do a sexy dance (naked)

💋 £10 = take it to the next level – you set the mark for this one!

*These are just suggestions for what might get your partner excited. If you're a terrible dancer (boys, pay attention) then you might want to come up with other ways to put on the ultimate peep show.

TITILLATING TIP

Use the money you earn to buy yourself some new sexy underwear or a sex toy for the bedroom, so you both feel the benefit!

LET'S GET

Physical

MUSICAL SEX CHAIRS

You will need

MUSIC THAT TURNS YOU ON
A REMOTE CONTROL FOR
YOUR MUSIC PLAYER
SOME CHAIRS

How to Play

NAUGHTINESS RATING 🩲 🩲

We all played the family-friendly version as kids, but cast aside any thoughts of winning a packet of chocolate buttons and prepare for things to get X-rated.

Play this one in your underwear. Turn the music up and get moving. Take it in turns to hold the remote control and when you feel your partner least expects it, pause the song and dash for the nearest chair. If you sit before they do, they must perform a lap dance for a minute before you pump the music up and you both get moving again. Remember to remove a chair to make the competition more fierce!

TITILLATING TIP

Play as dirty as you can! Distract your partner when it's their turn with the remote by flashing your best body parts, gyrating up against them and throwing them off their game.

BALL SKILLS

You will need

AN INDOOR GOLFING GREEN
A GOLF BALL
A PUTTER

* If you don't have an indoor golfing green you can always improvise with a plastic cup laid on its side (tape it down), or a flat ring-shaped object like a bangle in place of the hole.

How to Play

NAUGHTINESS RATING 🩲 🩲

Tee off! Take it in turns to run the golfing gauntlet.
Count how many putts it takes you to get the ball in
the hole. These equal the number of items of clothing
you must remove before your partner takes their turn.
The aim is to get the ball in the hole in as few shots as
possible – unless you're feeling like naked might be the
way to go... in that case, hit it into the rough.

RAUNCHY RULES

Whoever gets a hole-in-one not only wins the trophy (or
a bottle of bubbly you can both share!) but gets to call the
shots in the bedroom!

Titillating Tip

Dress up in your sexiest golf wear – girls, that means tight-fitting knits and mini shorts with over-the-knee socks; boys, golfing trousers with long socks and a tartan cap really does it for the ladies. Don't forget to stick your butt out when you're lining up the shot.

GOOD VIBRATIONS

You will need

A VIBRATING DEVICE

A BLINDFOLD

A POSTER-SIZED OUTLINE OF A HUMAN

BODY (NAUGHTY BITS INCLUDED)

A PEN

NAUGHTINESS RATING ▼ ▼ ▼

Blindfold your partner, turn them round three times and position them in front of the poster, which you've pinned up on the wall. They must then pick three places to tickle you (with the vibrator) to get you feeling frisky. Using the pen they must select these three body spots, and hope they've picked somewhere other than your big toe. Take the blindfold off them, and prepare to be tickled by the vibrator. Then it's their turn to feel the buzz!

RAUNCHY RULES

If they ask for help, don't give it (unless you're trying out the tip below). If they make marks on your elbow, or even off the poster, it's their fault if you don't feel in the mood to get it on.

Titillating Tip

Guide your partner as the pen moves over the picture of the human body by describing the parts of your body they're virtually touching. If there's a certain spot that gets you going make sure they stop there and for a change, demand they kiss/nibble/suck that spot instead.

HOLIDAY *Hot* SPOTS

THE LANGUAGE OF LUST

LOCALS LOVE IT WHEN PEOPLE FROM OUT OF TOWN TRY TO BLEND IN, SO RATHER THAN FLIRTING IN PLAIN OLD ENGLISH, WHICH YOU'RE PROBABLY A PRO AT ALREADY, WHY NOT TRY YOUR HAND AT A SPOT OF FOREIGN-SPEAK TO SPICE THINGS UP?

How to Play

NAUGHTINESS RATING ▼ ▼

Spend the afternoon hanging out with the cute bartender at your hotel pool. Get him to teach you all translations for a couple of come-ons that'll be sure to have you hooking up with the local boys and girls. Once you've practised on your friends, smarten yourself up and head off to the bars. Some possible one-liners you might want to learn are:

¿En qué lado de mi cama prefieres dormir? (Spanish)
Which side of my bed would you like to sleep on?

Tu es tellement chaude que tu fais fondre l'élastique de mon caleçon! (French)
You're so hot you melt the elastic in my underwear.

Scommetto venti euros che stai per darmi un due di picche. (Italian)
I bet you twenty quid you're going to turn me down.

For every successful pull (i.e. getting someone's number, a cheeky snog... or more!) you get a point. The boy or girl with the most points at the end of the night wins!

RAUNCHY RULES

A foreign chat-up line must be used at least once during each attempted pull. Another member of the group should hover close by to check no cheating is taking place.

TITILLATING TIP

Locals love to share their culture. So, once you've bagged a good 'un, get them to teach you a chat-up line or sexy phrase of their own. For every one you can successfully repeat (and translate back into English) for your mates, award yourself a bonus point.

I'M ALL FOR BRINGING BACK THE BIRCH, BUT ONLY BETWEEN CONSENTING ADULTS.

GORE VIDAL

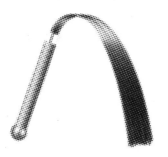

UP IN THE AIR

FLIGHTS CAN BE YAWNSOME AT THE
BEST OF TIMES — WHAT BETTER WAY
TO MAKE TIME LITERALLY FLY THAN BY
GETTING IN SOME HIGH-ALTITUDE HORNY
BEHAVIOUR WITH YOUR PARTNER OR
EVEN A HOT STRANGER, YES PLEASE!

How to Play

NAUGHTINESS RATING ▼ ▼ ▼

Make friends with the hottest person on your flight and switch seats so you're together – this could be a challenge in itself. Once you're settled and acquainted, explain the rules to them. The aim of the game is to orgasm on the flight. This can be achieved by any means necessary, but there are three golden rules that cannot be broken:

1 You cannot spend more than 5 minutes away from your seat.

2 You cannot tell anyone else what is going on.

3 You cannot get caught in the act.

4 If you're unable to get off onboard then you must buy your buddy a drink from the cart.

If you're seeing to yourself in the bathroom, your new friend's going to have to take you on trust. Why not snap a photo of you pleasuring yourself on your mobile phone to give him something sexy to look at.

TITILLATING TIP

A good way to ensure you're sitting next to your cutie is by befriending them at check-in. Get your seats allocated together, and start the banter before the plane's even taken off.

UNDERWATER LOVE

HOLIDAYS CAN BE LAZY TIMES, SO HEADING OUT INTO THE POOL OR THE SEA IS A GREAT WAY TO BURN OFF SOME OF THOSE ICE CREAMS. SPLASHING AROUND IN THE WAVES AND LOOKING LIKE A DROWNED RAT CAN BE DULL THOUGH, AND NOT PARTICULARLY SEXY, SO THIS GAME IS DESIGNED TO INJECT A BIT OF SAUCE INTO YOUR SWIM-TIME.

NAUGHTINESS RATING ▼ ▼ ▼

Only play this game on a day when (or in a place where) the waters are calm. Head out into the sea with your partner to a place where you can both comfortably stand on the seabed. Once you're deep enough, and most of your body is underwater, touch a part of your own body and ask your partner to guess where they think you're touching yourself. If they get it right, they get a kiss. Then, it's their turn.

RAUNCHY RULES

Kisses should increase in intensity and passion with each correct answer your partner provides.

Titillating Tip

Try leaving your swimwear on the beach and playing the game in the buff. All the touching will probably get you both so excited you'll be writhing around like horny sea lions on the sand before you know it!

PRIDE AND SEXINESS

WE'VE ALL SEEN THE MOMENT MR DARCY (AKA COLIN 'CHECK OUT MY CHEST HAIR' FIRTH) EMERGED FROM THE POND SOAKED THROUGH AND OH-SO-SEXY — IT'S TIME TO RECREATE THE MAGIC...

You will need

A PERIOD HOUSE WITH EXTENSIVE GARDENS
A PENCHANT FOR JANE AUSTEN-ESQUE DRAMAS
SOME OLDE-WORLDE COSTUMES (OPTIONAL)

How to Play

NAUGHTINESS RATING ▼ ▼ ▼

Head to one of the country's many beautiful period homes. Try not to talk to each other much on the journey there, and when you arrive get into character. Find secluded spots where young children and grannies feeding the ducks can't see you, and try out some of the following.

💋 Jump into the lake fully clothed and then emerge to passionately embrace your partner – OK, so this didn't happen in Austen, but they were right prudes back then!

💋 Pretend one of you is a lowly servant, the other a wealthy aristocrat in need of some lower-class action.

💋 After arguing with the person you secretly love while on a walk in the gardens, you get caught in a storm. Taking shelter in a nearby barn, you remove your clothes and immediately start getting it on. Ooh ah!

SUPERMARKET SWEEP

You will need

A SHOPPING LIST FOR EACH PLAYER

A WALLET WITH CASH IN IT

A LOCAL SUPERMARKET

NAUGHTINESS RATING 👙 👙

Write out a shopping list of items with sexual connotations, or that can be used for naughty games (including some in this book). Give a list to your partner and keep one for yourself. Head to your local supermarket and agree a meeting point somewhere outside. Screech 'Go!' and then it's the first person to find and purchase all the items and make it back to the meeting point who's the winner. Items must be bought, not stolen, borrowed or from your own personal collection of portable sexy things.

TITILLATING TIP

To make things extra fun, dress up for the sweep. Pick a sexy theme such as Moulin Rouge.

SEX ON THE BRAIN

GOING OUT FOR A ROMANTIC MEAL IS THE
BEST WAY TO SET THINGS IN MOTION
FOR A NIGHT OF HOT ADULT BEHAVIOUR,
BUT WHY WAIT TILL YOU'RE BACK HOME
BEFORE YOU GET YOUR PARTNER ALL
EXCITED? WHET THEIR APPETITE WITH
THIS SAUCY GAME AND THEY'LL PAY THE
BILL JUST TO GET YOU HOME FASTER!

NAUGHTINESS RATING ▼ ▼

Think of something really sexy. It could be your favourite
sexual position, a particular sexual encounter with your
partner, the part of their body you love the most, or
anything that turns you on. Once you have the thought in
your head your partner gets to ask you six sexy questions (to
which you can only answer yes or no) to try and decipher
what you're thinking. If they guess it right, then you have to
buy them dessert/a glass of wine/pay the bill, etc.

RAUNCHY RULES

Your partner has to trust that you're not changing your
mind to avoid buying them any after-dinner treats, so
don't be a sore loser – if they guess right, fess up!

Titillating Tip

Don't think that just because you're in a fancy public place touching is banned. Play footsie, and slowly run your fingers up and down your partner's hand to let them know you're thinking sexy thoughts.

SEX
Rated

SEXPIONAGE

You will need

A TRENCH COAT
A PAIR OF DARK GLASSES
A MOBILE PHONE

How to Play

NAUGHTINESS RATING ▼ ▼ ▼ ▼

The aim of the game is to successfully take something that belongs to your lover, while distracting them with your sheer sexiness. Tell them that if you are successful they have to take you out for dinner. You have one day to achieve this and must complete the following steps:

1 Send this text to your lover: 'We need to meet. You've been a bad boy/girl.' Arrange to meet at a restaurant or bar.

2 Wear a trench coat (with nothing but sexy undies underneath) and head out to meet them.

3 Arrive at your destination, sit with them and flash some flesh. Tell them you have something for them in the bathroom and they should follow you there in one minute.

4 When they arrive in the bathroom, remove your jacket and throw yourself on them. They won't be able to resist you.

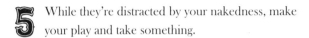

5 While they're distracted by your nakedness, make your play and take something.

6 Back at the table reveal your steal and get them to pay the bill. Hot sex and a free dinner – not bad for a day's work!

RAUNCHY RULES

Only you know all the steps and can know if you successfully completed them, so this is more a game for you and your libido than to be played as a pair. There's no need to actually steal anything from your lover, and you can return their property after they tell you how hot you were!

TITILLATING TIP

Be as much of an actor/actress as you can. Imagine yourself as a sexy spy (think *Mr & Mrs Smith*) and try to ignore any weird looks around you. Make sure your coat is fitted and sexy and that you don't look like a kid playing dress-up. You want your lover to be aroused by your antics, not amused.

WHEN I GET DOWN ON MY KNEES, IT'S NOT TO PRAY.

MADONNA

CHOO CHOO OOH

You will need

A NOTEPAD

A PEN

How to Play

NAUGHTINESS RATING 🩲 🩲 🩲

Commuting to work is one of the least sexy times of the day. No longer. Sit next to your partner on the train and obey the following rules:

1 When the train pulls into a station start kissing your partner. You can only stop when the train starts moving again.

2 If the train goes through a tunnel you must remove one item of clothing.

3 When the announcer says the name of your destination at any point during the journey you must touch each other as inappropriately as you dare.

4 If you visit the buffet car, or if a food cart comes by, you must order a *hot* coffee and a *warm* muffin.

If your partner fails to comply with any of the rules, you have permission to flirt outrageously with your fellow commuters until they complete the next task.

TITILLATING TIP

Make up your own rules so the journey is even sexier – such as 'no-underwear Mondays', 'talk-dirty Tuesdays', 'wet-shirt Wednesdays', 'touch-me-up Thursdays' and 'fumble Fridays'!

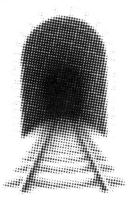

HOT UNDER THE COLLAR

You will need

A WEDDING TO ATTEND (NOT YOURS!)
A BRIGHT/DISTINCTIVE LIPSTICK

NAUGHTINESS RATING 🩲 🩲 🩲

Speeches, bad music, awkward conversation with elderly relatives – yes, weddings can be dull, but they're also a hotbed for well-dressed, horny singles looking for some action, i.e. the perfect setting to get hot under the collar. This game should be played by a group of willing ladies. Apply a healthy layer of lipstick and head to the reception. The aim of the game is to mark as many shirt collars as you can with your lipstick. You get one point for every man you tag on the collar. At the end of the night, if your fuzzy head allows it, calculate who scored the most points and reward them with an extra-large helping of wedding cake. Yum!

Raunchy Rules

The following bonus points should be awarded:

💋 Every buttonhole flower you steal = 2 points

💋 Every tie or bowtie you manage to swipe = 5 points

💋 Anyone who finishes the night wearing a top hat = 10 points

💋 Photographic evidence of your lipstick on a man's chest = 15 points

SU-DO-ME-KU

DO YOU HAVE A PARTNER WHO SPENDS FAR MORE TIME STUDYING THAN STUDYING YOU? THIS GAME WILL REDRESS THE BALANCE AND MAKE SURE YOU'RE ALL THEY'VE GOT THEIR EYES ON.

You will need

A SUDOKU PUZZLE
A PEN
SPARKLING WINE

How to Play

NAUGHTINESS RATING ▼ ▼ ▼ ▼ ▼

Take a simple game of sudoku (it helps if you know
how to play this game first) and hand it to your partner
– make sure you pick one that's not too easy for them.
Each correct number that they insert into the puzzle
corresponds to something you're going to do. Each time
they insert a new number you stop doing the previous
action and continue with a different one. You must keep
performing the act until they insert a different number.
If they insert a:

1, 2 or 3: you will strut around in nothing but your
underwear.

4, 5 or 6: you will take off an item of their clothing.

7, 8 or 9: you will pour sparkling wine down yourself
and let them lick it off.

Raunchy Rules

If they complete the entire puzzle in under 15 minutes (not that it will be easy for them with you frolicking around in the buff), then they should be rewarded with some *very* hot sex.

TITILLATING TIP

If your partner's struggling to complete the puzzle they're allowed to ask you for help, but only once. If you correctly insert a number they have to put the puzzle down, take off their clothes and give you a back rub in the buff.

NB: If you're more into puzzles than your partner, no worries, the roles can easily be reversed!

DON'T SWEAT IT

You will need

SEXY GYM KIT

NAUGHTINESS RATING ▼ ▼ ▼ ▼

It's great seeing your partner get all hot and sweaty, so where better to play this game than down at the gym. To win this game you have to prove your sexy status in three different stages.

Stage 1: Warm-Up
Kit yourself out in your sexiest gym wear and run side by side on two treadmills. After each minute of running passes you must both make a sexy remark to your partner. It can be anything as long as it includes one of the following words: sex, body, hot, dirty, sweat. But the sexier you can make it, the hotter you'll both start to feel. You must both say your sentences within 10 seconds of the minute passing, so keep an eye on your treadmill timer to make sure you're being quick enough. Keep going until one of you can't think of a remark in the time limit. The other person is the winner of Stage 1 and scores 1 point.

Stage 2: Cool Down

Head to the mats to do some stretching. Take it in turns to decide on a stretch position for both of you. When you are stretching you have to make groaning sex noises; start quietly, and get progressively louder (you must make a louder noise than the one your partner just made). The loser is whoever cracks first. Score 1 point for winning.

Stage 3: Sauna

There's no point going to the gym if you're not going to get all sweaty and naked in the sauna. Whoever dares to bare all scores a point for this stage. You can both score points if you're both feeling like flashing the flesh.

RAUNCHY RULES

The winner is whoever scores the most points. Their reward? How about one of these:

- A relaxing back rub back home

- A steamy shower they won't forget in a hurry

- A glass of wine and a sexy bubble bath

Bonus points! If either you or your partner gets chatted up by someone during the gym session take home an extra point (and maybe someone else's number!).

IF YOU USE THE ELECTRIC VIBRATOR NEAR WATER, YOU WILL COME AND GO AT THE SAME TIME.

LOUISE SAMMONS

Have Fun!

If you're interested in finding out more about our books, find us on Facebook at **SUMMERSDALE PUBLISHERS** and follow us on Twitter at **@SUMMERSDALE**.

WWW.SUMMERSDALE.COM